READY, STEADY, PRACTISE!

Paul Broadbent

Mental Arithmetic
Pupil Book **Year 5**

Features of this book

- Clear explanations and worked examples for each mental arithmetic topic from the KS2 National Curriculum.

- Questions split into three sections that become progressively more challenging:

Warm up

Test yourself

Challenge yourself

- 'How did you do?' checks at the end of each topic for self-evaluation.

- Regular progress tests to assess pupils' understanding and recap on their learning.

- Answers to every question in a pull-out section at the centre of the book.

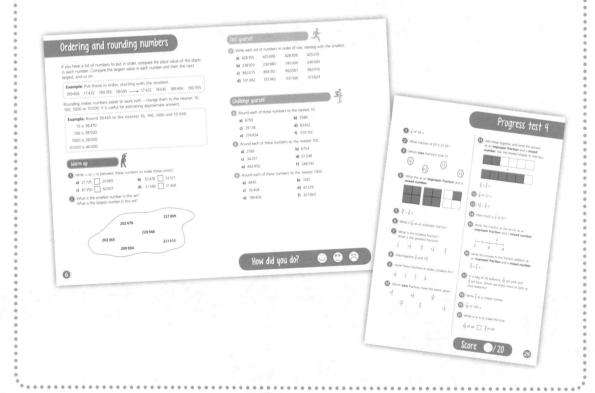

Contents

Counting and place value

Look at this number and how it is made.

817 265 = 800 000 + 10 000 + 7000 + 200 + 60 + 5

eight hundred and seventeen thousand two hundred and sixty-five

Hundred thousands	Ten thousands	Thousands	Hundreds	Tens	Ones
8	1	7	2	6	5

800 000 ＞ 10 000 ＞ 7000 ＞ 200 ＞ 60 ＞ 5

Look at the difference between numbers to work out the size of each step in a pattern.

-7 -7 -7 -7

725 718 711 704 ___   This is going down in sevens. The next number is 697.

Warm up

1) Work out the missing numbers.

   a) 72 195   = 70 000 + 2000 + _____ + _____ + _____

   b) 46 355   = _____ + _____ + _____ + 50 + 5

   c) 149 837 = 100 000 + _____ + _____ + _____ + 30 + _____

   d) 283 954 = _____ + _____ + _____ + _____ + _____ + 4

   e) 723 593 = _____ + 20 000 + _____ + _____ + _____ + _____

2) Copy each sequence and write the missing numbers.

   a)   108   158   _____   258   _____   358   _____

   b)   _____   _____   6405   6505   6605   _____   6805

   c)   18   _____   4   −3   _____   _____   −24

   d)   7855   7825   7795   _____   _____   7705   _____

   e)   −35   −20   _____   _____   _____   40   55

3 Two numbers in each sequence have been swapped over.
What are the two numbers?

a) 480   478   468   474   472   470   476

b) 3165   3150   3155   3160   3145   3170   3175

c) 1144   1124   1136   1132   1128   1140   1120

4 a) What number is 5000 more than 26 145?

b) What number is 10 000 more than 85 035?

c) What number is 50 000 less than 178 360?

d) What number is 20 000 less than 34 223?

5 What are the missing numbers for this multiplication machine?

IN	234		93		345
OUT		30 000		41 000	

2024 is the halfway number between 2016 and 2032.

2016 ------ 2024 ------ 2032

6 What are the halfway numbers between these numbers?

a) 42 440 _____ 42 880   b) −34 _____ −6

c) 60 038 _____ 61 038   d) 91 458 _____ 95 458

How did you do?   ☹

Ordering and rounding numbers

If you have a list of numbers to put in order, compare the place value of the digits in each number. Compare the largest value in each number and then the next largest, and so on.

> **Example: Put these in order, starting with the smallest.**
>
> 189 456   17 432   190 355   18 045 ⟶   17 432   18 045   189 456   190 355

Rounding makes numbers easier to work with – change them to the nearest 10, 100, 1000 or 10 000. It is useful for estimating approximate answers.

> **Example: Round 238 465 to the nearest 10, 100, 1000, 10 000 and 100 000**
>
> 10 is 238 470
>
> 100 is 238 500
>
> 1000 is 238 000
>
> 10 000 is 240 000
>
> 100 000 is 200 000

Warm up

1 Write < or > in between these numbers to make these correct.

a) 21 735 ☐ 20 889

b) 53 478 ☐ 53 521

c) 61 350 ☐ 62 007

d) 31 486 ☐ 31 468

2 What is the smallest number in this set?
What is the largest number in this set?

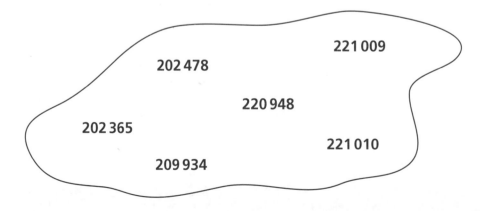

202 478

221 009

220 948

202 365

221 010

209 934

3 Write each set of numbers in order of size, starting with the smallest.

a) 428 355 _4_   425 009 _1_   428 309 _3_   425 010 _2_

b) 238 970 _2_   230 980 _1_   245 000 _4_   240 500 _3_

c) 863 015 _1_   866 351 _4_   863 501 _2_   863 510 _3_

d) 531 962 _4_   513 962 _2_   531 926 _3_   513 629 _1_

Challenge yourself

4 Round each of these numbers to the nearest 10.

a) 6793   b) 3586   c) 29 136

d) 83 452   e) 276 834   f) 579 35

5 Round each of these numbers to the nearest 100.

a) 2186   b) 6754   c) 34 257

d) 61 548   e) 843 956   f) 286 541

6 Round each of these numbers to the nearest 1000.

a) 4845   b) 7487   c) 36 404

d) 43 529   e) 189 456   f) 207 863

7 Round each of these numbers to the nearest 10 000.

a) 11 325   b) 22 645   c) 59 777

d) 96 892   e) 276 580   f) 823 470

8 Round each of these numbers to the nearest 100 000.

a) 105 680   b) 385 257   c) 515 830

d) 732 713   e) 895 900   f) 943 666

How did you do?

Addition

Use any facts you know to help you learn others.

Example: 8 + 6 = 14

You can use this to work out these and other facts.

$$18 + 16 = 34 \qquad\qquad 80 + 60 = 140$$
$$1800 + 1600 = 3400 \qquad\qquad 800 + 600 = 1400$$
$$4080 + 3060 = 7140 \qquad\qquad 5008 + 1006 = 6014$$

Warm up

1 Work out these sums:

Use the first answer to help with the others in each set.

a) $7 + 6$ =

$70 + 60$ = $700 + 600$ =

$1007 + 3006$ = $2070 + 4060$ =

b) $9 + 5$ =

$90 + 50$ = $900 + 500$ =

$49 + 25$ = $1090 + 6050$ =

c) $3 + 8$ =

$30 + 80$ = $300 + 800$ =

$6300 + 2800$ = $4030 + 3080$ =

d) $8 + 7$ =

$80 + 70$ = $800 + 700$ =

$58 + 37$ = $3080 + 2070$ =

2 Work out the missing numbers on these addition walls. Each missing number is the sum of the two numbers below.

a)

b)

c)

d)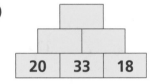

e)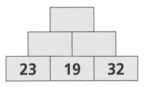

f)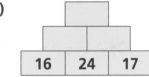

3 Look at these numbers and answer the questions.

1405   2002   2404   3003

a) Add together the two odd numbers.

b) What is the total of the two smallest numbers?

c) Add together the two even numbers.

d) What is the total of the two largest numbers?

e) Work out the total of the three largest numbers.

Challenge yourself

4 Look at these two 4-digit additions.

1234 + 8765 = 9999   **3333 + 6666 = 9999**

Find four more 4-digit additions that total 9999.

How did you do?

Subtraction

There are different strategies you can use to subtract mentally.

Counting on from the smallest number is a good method.

Example: **What is 320 subtract 170?**

Count on from 170 to
200 and then to 320.

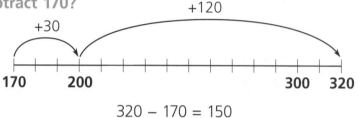

$$320 - 170 = 150$$

You could try breaking the numbers up so that you can subtract them in your head.

Example: **Take away 150 from 192.**

$$192 - 150 =$$

$$190 + 2 - 150 =$$

$$190 - 150 + 2 = 40 + 2 = 42$$

Warm up

1. Use the number lines to help you subtract these mentally.

a)

180 200   270

$$270 - 180 =$$

b)

240   300   410

$$410 - 240 =$$

c)

180   200   300   325

$$325 - 180 =$$

d)

250   300   345

$$345 - 250 =$$

e)

270   300   400   455

$$455 - 270 =$$

2 Answer these.

a) Take 35 away from 92.

b) Subtract 130 from 208.

c) What is 49 less than 120?

d) Take away 63 from 101.

e) What is 121 take away 97?

3 Look at these numbers and answer the questions.

1200　　　**3100**　　　**2800**　　　**3900**

a) Which two numbers have a difference of 300?

b) Which number is 100 less than 4000?

c) Which two numbers have a difference of 1600?

Challenge yourself

4 What are the missing numbers for each subtraction machine?

a)

IN → −240 → OUT

IN	330	500	410	365	315	405
OUT	90					

b)

IN → −380 → OUT

IN	570	640	410	500	730	620
OUT						

How did you do?

Addition and subtraction problems

Look out for addition and subtraction words in any problems. They can give a clue for how to solve the problem.

Addition words

add, total, altogether, sum, plus, more than, increase

Subtraction words

subtract, take away, minus, less than, fewer, difference, reduce

Be careful though, some problems are confusing. Read them carefully and 'picture' the problem.

Warm up

1 Work these to find out how much is left for each one.

a) A jug holds 1200 ml of orange juice. 750 ml is poured into one glass and 350 ml into another glass.

How much orange juice is left?

b) Megan buys 5500 mm of cloth. She cuts off a piece 1400 mm long to make a skirt and cuts another piece of 2500 mm to make a scarf.

How much cloth is left over?

c) Mrs Wise buys a 3200 g box of washing powder. She gives 1800 g to her sister and uses 900 g herself.

How much washing powder is left in the box?

d) A farmer collects 370 eggs one week and 420 the next week. He has to throw 35 away as they were cracked.

How many eggs does he have left to take to market?

2 These are the lengths of some of the longest rivers in the world, rounded to the nearest 10 km. Answer the questions that follow.

River	Continent	Length
Nile	Africa	6690 km
Amazon	S. America	6380 km
Mississippi	N. America	6270 km
Chang Jiang	Asia	6210 km

a) What is the difference in length between the two longest rivers in the world, the Nile and the Amazon?

b) Which river is 480 km shorter than the Nile?

c) Which two rivers have a difference in length of 420 km?

3 A school is collecting bottle tops for recycling. It is aiming for a target of 3000 bottle tops. These are the totals for the first three months:

Month	Bottle tops collected
January	800
February	690
March	710

How many more bottle tops does the school need to collect to reach its target?

4 Two boxes of paper have a difference in weight of 3600 g. When they are put together, they have a total weight of 6400 g.

What is the weight of each box of paper?

How did you do?

1 Round each number to the nearest 10.

58 834

927 015

2 Write in words the value of the underlined digit.

490 152

3 Multiply both numbers by 1000.

26   519

4 What is the smallest number? What is the largest number?

32 607   27 036   30 762

26 703   32 076

5 Write the halfway number between these two numbers.

−25 _____ −5

6 What is the missing number?

5195   5095 _____   4895   4795

7 Write two hundred and sixty-one thousand four hundred and ten in numerals.

8 What number is 6000 less than 988 799?

9 Work out the next number in this sequence.

44 372   44 272   44 172 _____

10 Make the smallest possible 5-digit number using these digit cards.

7   8   2

1   3

11 What number is 30 000 more than 214 503?

12 Copy and write < or > between these numbers to make this correct.

895 135 ☐ 895 513 ☐ 893 555

13 Count in 1000s. Work out the two missing numbers.

58 820 _____ _____ 61 820

14 Work out the missing numbers.

−43   −23 _____ _____   37

15 Write in words the value of the underlined digit.

5 706 289

16 Round each number to the nearest 1000.

17 465

332 960

17 Write in words the value of the underlined digit.

917 264

18 Multiply both numbers by 100.

2054   631

19 Copy and write < or > between these numbers to make this correct.

46 743 ☐ 467 343

20 Work out the next two numbers in this sequence.

18   10   2 _____ _____

Score ◯ / 20

Progress test 2

1 320 − 280 =

2 Answer these additions.

40 + 70 =

3400 + 2700 =

3 A school has 560 children. 285 are girls. How many boys are there?

4 What is 100 less than 6000?

5 What is the total of 1490 and 6204?

6 Take 45 away from 80.

7 Two parcels weigh 2800 g and 1300 g. What is the total weight of the parcels?

8 56 + 28 =

These are the amounts of water used by one person in one year. Use these amounts to answer questions 9 and 10.

Daily normal shower = 2200 litres

Daily power shower = 8030 litres

9 How much less water is used over a year using a normal shower than a power shower?

10 How much water would two people use over a year if they had a normal shower every day?

11 Which is the odd one out?

6473 + 1304   5281 + 3607
2764 + 5013   4025 + 3752

12 What is 108 take away 94?

13 415 − 350 =

14 3008 + 2005 =

15 1450 ml of milk is used from a 2500 ml jug. How much milk is left in the jug?

16 Add together 2003, 5406 and 1401.

17 Which two numbers have a difference of 1500?

6500   7200
5700   6200   5100

18 430 − 280 =

19 27 + 43 =

20 A train travels 635 km from London to Edinburgh. How far is the return journey there and back again?

Score ⬤/20

15

Multiples, factors and primes

A **multiple** of a whole number is produced by multiplying that number by another whole number.

	×1	×2	×3	×4	×5	×6...	×20...	×100...
Multiples of 3 →	3	6	9	**12**	15	18...	60...	300...
Multiples of 4 →	4	8	**12**	16	20	24...	80...	400...

12 is a multiple of both 3 and 4.

This means that 12 is a **common multiple** of 3 and 4.

Factors of a number can divide that number exactly.

Factors of 15 ⟶ $15 = 1 \times 15$ $15 = 3 \times 5$

In order: 1, 3, 5, 15 In pairs: (1, 15), (3, 5)

Factors of 18 ⟶ $18 = 1 \times 18$ $18 = 2 \times 9$ $18 = 3 \times 6$

In order: 1, 2, 3, 6, 9, 18 In pairs: (1, 18), (2, 9), (3, 6)

This means that 1 and 3 are **common factors** of 15 and 18.

A **prime number** has only two factors: 1 and itself.

2, 3, 5, 7 and 11 are the first five prime numbers.

Warm up

1. Copy this Venn diagram, then write the numbers in the correct part. There are two numbers that do not fit on the diagram.

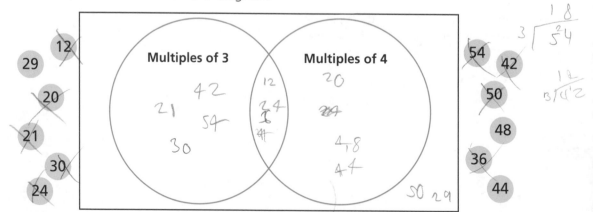

2 Choose from the circled numbers to find the correct answer for each of these.

a) A common multiple of 3 and 5 is: (35) (45) (55)

b) A common multiple of 2 and 3 is: (28) (38) (48)

c) A common multiple of 5 and 6 is: (70) (80) (90)

d) A common multiple of 3 and 10 is: (100) (120) (160)

3 Write the factors of these numbers in pairs.

a) 27 **b)** 60 **c)** 42 **d)** 48

4 Use these numbers to answer each question.

12	8	9	5

a) Which number is a factor of 64? **b)** Which number is a factor of 35?

c) Which two numbers are factors of 36? **d)** Which two numbers are factors of 60?

5 What are the common factors of 12 and 9?

6 **a)** Work out the factors of these prime numbers and square numbers.
Write the factors for each number in order.

Prime numbers

19 ⟶ 1 19

23 ⟶ 1 23

5 ⟶ 1 5

37 ⟶ 1 37

Square numbers

16 ⟶ 16 8 4 2 1

9 ⟶ 1 3 9

25 ⟶ 1 5 25

36 ⟶ 1 2 3 4 6
          9 18 36 12

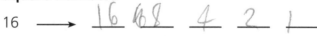

b) What do you notice about the number of factors for prime numbers?

c) What do you notice about the number of factors for square numbers?

How did you do?

Multiplication

Use the tables facts that you know to help you multiply bigger numbers.

> **8 × 4 = 32**
>
> **80 × 40 = 3200**

Partition numbers and mentally calculate each part to make them easier to work with.

> Follow these steps to answer 83 multiplied by 4:
>
> 83 × 4 is the same as 80 × 4 added to 3 × 4
>
> 320 + 12 = 332
>
> So, 83 × 4 = 332

Warm up

1 Answer these multiplications.

a) 7 × 9   =

   70 × 90 =

b) 6 × 3   =

   60 × 30 =

c) 8 × 6   =

   80 × 60 =

d) 9 × 9   =

   90 × 90 =

e) 7 × 8   =

   70 × 80 =

f) 9 × 12   =

   90 × 120 =

2 Copy and complete this multiplication grid.

×	32	54	45
6			
3			
8			

3 Answer these multiplications.

a) 46 × 3 =   **b)** 39 × 5 =   **c)** 28 × 6 =

d) 54 × 4 =   **e)** 81 × 3 =   **f)** 65 × 8 =

4 Multiply these sets of three numbers.

a)   **b)**

c)   **d)**

Challenge yourself

5 Look at the three digits below.

Arrange them to make multiplications like this:

9 **6** × **5** = 480

a) Arrange the digits to make the largest product.

b) Arrange the digits to make the smallest product.

c) Arrange the digits to make the product as close as possible to 500.

How did you do?

Division

Break numbers up to help you work out division answers.

Example: What is 94 divided by 4?

Break 94 up into 80 and 14.

$$80 \div 4 = 20$$
$$14 \div 4 = 3 \text{ r } 2$$
$$\text{So } 94 \div 4 = 23 \text{ r } 2$$

When there is a remainder it can be represented in different ways.

$94 \div 4 = 23 \text{ r } 2$ **or...** $94 \div 4 = 23\frac{1}{2}$ **or...** $94 \div 4 = 23.5$

Warm up

1 What are the missing numbers? Use your multiplication and division facts to help you answer each one.

a) $27 \div \underline{\hphantom{00}} = 3$

b) $28 \div 4 = \underline{\hphantom{00}}$

c) $\underline{\hphantom{00}} \div 9 = 4$

d) $24 \div 8 = \underline{\hphantom{00}}$

e) $49 \div \underline{\hphantom{00}} = 7$

f) $\underline{\hphantom{00}} \div 3 = 6$

g) $27 \div 9 = \underline{\hphantom{00}}$

h) $54 \div \underline{\hphantom{00}} = 6$

i) $56 \div 7 = \underline{\hphantom{00}}$

j) $\underline{\hphantom{00}} \div 12 = 8$

k) $110 \div 11 = \underline{\hphantom{00}}$

l) $\underline{\hphantom{00}} \div 6 = 12$

2 Answer these divisions.

    a) 96 ÷ 4 =   **b)** 105 ÷ 5 =

    c) 93 ÷ 3 =   **d)** 84 ÷ 6 =

    e) 112 ÷ 7 =   **f)** 112 ÷ 4 =

    g) 126 ÷ 6 =   **h)** 153 ÷ 3 =

3 Answer these divisions and show the remainders in three different ways.

    a) 47 ÷ 4 =   **b)** 83 ÷ 5 =

    c) 91 ÷ 2 =   **d)** 97 ÷ 10 =

    e) 69 ÷ 4 =   **f)** 99 ÷ 5 =

4 What are the missing numbers for each division machine?

    a)

IN	1100	3300	7700	9900	11 000	13 200
OUT	100					

    b)

IN	4800	2400	6000	9600	12 000	14 400
OUT						

How did you do?

Fractions

If the numerator is smaller than the denominator, it is known as a **proper fraction**. The value of each fraction is less than 1, e.g.

$$\frac{1}{6} \qquad \frac{3}{4} \qquad \frac{7}{10}$$

If the numerator is larger than the denominator, it is known as an **improper fraction**. The value of each fraction is greater than 1, e.g.

$$\frac{3}{2} \qquad \frac{7}{4} \qquad \frac{10}{7}$$

This shows seven slices of melon.
Each slice is $\frac{1}{4}$ of a whole melon.

There is one whole melon and $\frac{3}{4}$ of a melon.

$\frac{4}{4} + \frac{3}{4} = \frac{7}{4}$ or $1\frac{3}{4}$

$\frac{7}{4}$ is an **improper fraction**. $1\frac{3}{4}$ is a **mixed number**.

Warm up

1 Write each set of shapes as mixed numbers **and** improper fractions.

a)

b)

c)

d)

Answers

Pages 4–5
1. **a)** 100, 90, 5
   b) 40 000, 6000, 300
   c) 40 000, 9000, 800, 7
   d) 200 000, 80 000, 3000, 900, 50
   e) 700 000, 3000, 500, 90, 3
2. **a)** 208, 308, 408 **b)** 6205, 6305, 6705
   c) 11, –10, –17 **d)** 7765, 7735, 7675
   e) –5, 10, 25
3. **a)** 468, 476 **b)** 3165, 3145 **c)** 1124, 1140
4. **a)** 31 145 **b)** 95 035 **c)** 128 360 **d)** 14 223
5. Top row should be completed as follows: 30, 41
   Bottom row should be completed as follows:
   234 000, 93 000, 345 000
6. **a)** 42 660 **b)** –20 **c)** 60 538 **d)** 93 458

Pages 6–7
1. **a)** > **b)** < **c)** < **d)** >
2. 202 365, 221 010
3. **a)** 425 009, 425 010, 428 309, 428 355
   b) 230 980, 238 970, 240 500, 245 000
   c) 863 015, 863 501, 863 510, 866 351
   d) 513 629, 513 962, 531 926, 531 962
4. **a)** 6790 **b)** 3590 **c)** 29 140
   d) 83 450 **e)** 276 830 **f)** 579 360
5. **a)** 2200 **b)** 6800 **c)** 34 300
   d) 61 500 **e)** 844 000 **f)** 286 500
6. **a)** 5000 **b)** 7000 **c)** 36 000
   d) 44 000 **e)** 189 000 **f)** 208 000
7. **a)** 10 000 **b)** 20 000 **c)** 60 000
   d) 100 000 **e)** 280 000 **f)** 820 000
8. **a)** 100 000 **b)** 400 000 **c)** 500 000
   d) 700 000 **e)** 900 000 **f)** 900 000

Pages 8–9
1. **a)** 13, 130, 1300, 4013, 6130
   b) 14, 140, 1400, 74, 7140
   c) 11, 110, 1100, 9100, 7110
   d) 15, 150, 1500, 95, 5150
2. **a)** 64 **b)** 90 **c)** 81
   d) 104, 53, 51 **e)** 93, 42, 51 **f)** 81, 40, 41
3. **a)** 4408 **b)** 3407 **c)** 4406
   d) 5407 **e)** 7409
4. There are many possible answers. Check all
   additions total 9999.

Pages 10–11
1. **a)** 90 **b)** 170 **c)** 145 **d)** 95 **e)** 185
2. **a)** 57 **b)** 78 **c)** 71 **d)** 38 **e)** 24
3. **a)** 3100 and 2800 **b)** 3900 **c)** 1200 and 2800
4. **a)** Bottom row should be completed as follows:
       260, 170, 125, 75, 165
   b) Bottom row should be completed as follows:
       190, 260, 30, 120, 350, 240

Pages 12–13
1. **a)** 100 ml **b)** 1600 mm **c)** 500 g **d)** 755
2. **a)** 310 km **b)** Chang Jiang
   c) Nile and Mississippi

3. 800
4. 1400 g, 5000 g

Page 14
1. 58 830, 927 020
2. four hundred thousand
3. 26 000, 519 000
4. 26 703, 32 607
5. –15
6. 4995
7. 261 410
8. 982 799
9. 44 072
10. 12 378
11. 244 503
12. <, >
13. 59 820, 60 820
14. –3, 17
15. seven hundred thousand
16. 17 000, 333 000
17. seven thousand
18. 205 400, 63 100
19. <
20. –6, –14

Page 15
1. 40
2. 110, 6100
3. 275
4. 5900
5. 7694
6. 35
7. 4100 g
8. 84
9. 5830 litres
10. 4400 litres
11. 5281 + 3607
12. 14
13. 65
14. 5013
15. 1050 ml
16. 8810
17. 5700 and 7200
18. 150
19. 70
20. 1270 km

Pages 16–17
1.

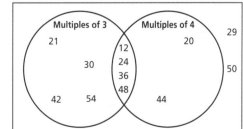

Answers

2. a) 45 **b)** 48 **c)** 90 **d)** 120
3. a) (1, 27), (3, 9)
b) (1, 60), (2, 30), (3, 20), (4, 15), (5, 12), (6, 10)
c) (1, 42), (2, 21), (3, 14), (6, 7)
d) (1, 48), (2, 24), (3, 16), (4, 12), (6, 8)
4. a) 8 **b)** 5 **c)** 12, 9 **d)** 12, 5
5. 1 and 3
6. a) Prime numbers:
$19 \rightarrow 1, 19; 23 \rightarrow 1, 23;$
$5 \rightarrow 1, 5; 37 \rightarrow 1, 37$
Square numbers:
$16 \rightarrow 1, 2, 4, 8, 16$
$9 \rightarrow 1, 3, 9$
$25 \rightarrow 1, 5, 25$
$36 \rightarrow 1, 2, 3, 4, 6, 9, 12, 18, 36$
b) There are only two factors.
c) There is an odd number of factors.

Pages 18–19
1. a) 63, 6300 **b)** 18, 1800 **c)** 48, 4800
d) 81, 8100 **e)** 56, 5600 **f)** 108, 10800
2.

×	32	54	45
6	192	324	270
3	96	162	135
8	256	432	360

3. a) 138 **b)** 195 **c)** 168 **d)** 216
e) 243 **f)** 520
4. a) 252 **b)** 240 **c)** 432 **d)** 168
5. a) $65 \times 9 = 585$ **b)** $69 \times 5 = 345$ **c)** $56 \times 9 = 504$

Pages 20–21
1. a) 9 **b)** 7 **c)** 36 **d)** 3 **e)** 7 **f)** 18
g) 3 **h)** 9 **i)** 8 **j)** 96 **k)** 10 **l)** 72
2. a) 24 **b)** 21 **c)** 31 **d)** 14 **e)** 16
f) 28 **g)** 21 **h)** 51
3. a) 11 r 3 or $11\frac{3}{4}$ or 11.75 **b)** 16 r 3 or $16\frac{3}{5}$ or 16.6
c) 45 r 1 or $45\frac{1}{2}$ or 45.5 **d)** 9 r 7 or $9\frac{7}{10}$ or 9.7
e) 17 r 1 or $17\frac{1}{4}$ or 17.25 **f)** 19 r 4 or $19\frac{4}{5}$ or 19.8
4. a) Bottom row should be completed as follows:
300, 700, 900, 1000, 1200
b) Bottom row should be completed as follows:
400, 200, 500, 800, 1000, 1200

Pages 22–23
1. a) $1\frac{2}{3}, \frac{5}{3}$ **b)** $3\frac{1}{2}, \frac{7}{2}$ **c)** $2\frac{3}{5}, \frac{13}{5}$ **d)** $2\frac{1}{6}, \frac{13}{6}$
2. a) $\frac{9}{4}$ **b)** $\frac{13}{3}$ **c)** $\frac{13}{8}$ **d)** $\frac{15}{4}$
e) $\frac{12}{5}$ **f)** $\frac{7}{6}$
3. a) $1\frac{1}{2}$ **b)** $1\frac{1}{4}$ **c)** $3\frac{1}{3}$ **d)** $1\frac{1}{7}$
e) $7\frac{1}{2}$ **f)** $5\frac{1}{3}$
4. A $1\frac{3}{4}, \frac{7}{4}$ **B** $2\frac{1}{4}, \frac{9}{4}$ **C** $2\frac{1}{2}, \frac{5}{2}$ **D** $3\frac{1}{4}, \frac{13}{4}$
E $3\frac{3}{4}, \frac{15}{4}$

5. $2\frac{1}{4}, \frac{12}{4}, \frac{14}{4}, 3\frac{3}{4}, 4\frac{1}{2}, \frac{11}{2}$

Pages 24–25
1. a) $\frac{1}{3}$ **b)** $\frac{1}{2}$
c) $\frac{1}{3}$ **d)** $\frac{1}{6}$
2. a) < **b)** <
c) > **d)** <
3. a) $\frac{1}{2}, \frac{1}{5}, \frac{1}{10}, \frac{1}{4}, \frac{3}{4}$ **b)** $\frac{1}{10}, \frac{1}{2}, \frac{1}{4}, \frac{3}{4}, \frac{1}{5}$
c) $\frac{1}{4}, \frac{1}{2}, \frac{1}{10}, \frac{3}{4}, \frac{1}{5}$
4. a) $\frac{1}{10}$ of 10 kg **b)** thirds
c) more time sleeping **d)** more spotted fish

Pages 26–27
1. $1\frac{3}{4}, 1\frac{1}{4}$
$2\frac{3}{10}, \frac{7}{10}$
$1\frac{7}{8}, 1\frac{1}{8}$
$2\frac{1}{3}, \frac{2}{3}$
$1\frac{1}{3}, 1\frac{2}{3}$
2. a) $\frac{8}{4}$ (or 2) **b)** $\frac{6}{10}$ (or $\frac{3}{5}$) **c)** $\frac{9}{5}$ (or $1\frac{4}{5}$) **d)** $\frac{8}{10}$ (or $\frac{4}{5}$)
3. a) $\frac{6}{4}$ or $1\frac{1}{2}$ **b)** $\frac{7}{6}$ or $1\frac{1}{6}$ **c)** $\frac{11}{10}$ or $1\frac{1}{10}$ **d)** $\frac{6}{5}$ or $1\frac{1}{5}$
4. a) $\frac{2}{4}$ or $\frac{1}{2}$ **b)** $\frac{2}{3}$
5. a) $\frac{7}{10}$ **b)** $\frac{1}{8}$
6. a) 7 **b)** $\frac{6}{10}$ m (or $\frac{3}{5}$ m) **c)** $\frac{8}{9}$ **d)** $\frac{5}{12}$ litres

Page 28
1. 17 **2.** 7 **3.** (3, 6) **4.** 54, 5400
5. 140 **6.** 27.5 **7.** 8000 **8.** 21
9. 4 **10.** 2800 **11.** 60 **12.** 3
13. 371 **14.** 4 **15.** > **16.** 120
17. $14\frac{2}{5}$ **18.** 12 **19.** 8 **20.** 4

Page 29
1. 4 **2.** $\frac{1}{4}$
3. $1\frac{1}{2}$ and $3\frac{1}{2}$ **4.** $\frac{9}{4}, 2\frac{1}{4}$
5. $\frac{11}{4}$ (or $2\frac{3}{4}$) **6.** $\frac{27}{10}$
7. $1\frac{1}{3}, \frac{8}{3}$ **8.** 5
9. $\frac{1}{10}, \frac{1}{7}, \frac{1}{4}, \frac{1}{2}$ **10.** $1\frac{4}{5}, \frac{9}{5}$
11. $\frac{7}{6}$ or $1\frac{1}{6}$ **12.** 9
13. $\frac{7}{9}$ **14.** 20p
15. $\frac{5}{2}, 2\frac{1}{2}$ **16.** $\frac{14}{9}$ or $1\frac{5}{9}$
17. more blue balloons **18.** $1\frac{2}{3}$
19. 84 **20.** <

Pages 30–31
1. a) 3.4 **b)** 86 **c)** 12.28 **d)** 8.55
e) 37.2 **f)** 16.2
2. a) 8.35 **b)** 1.9 **c)** 22.76 **d)** 2.845
e) 0.093 **f)** 1.284
3. a) 368 **b)** 30 **c)** 100.5 **d)** 293.4
e) 65.5 **f)** 4638.5

4. a) 0.27 b) 3.42
  c) 0.538 d) 0.063
  e) 0.279 f) 1.452

5. 0.855 kg, 0.95 kg, 8.245 kg, 8.3 kg, 8.455 kg, 8.52 kg

6. a) 3.3 b) 3.8 c) 3.1 d) 3.6
  e) 3.9 f) 3.4

Pages 32–33

1. a) 50% b) 25% c) 10% d) 20%
  e) 60% f) 72% g) 58% h) 65%
  i) 80% j) 30% k) 34% l) 55%

2. a) $\frac{1}{10}$ b) $\frac{4}{5}$ c) $\frac{1}{2}$ d) $\frac{3}{10}$
  e) $\frac{3}{5}$ f) $\frac{1}{4}$ g) $\frac{1}{20}$ h) $\frac{9}{10}$
  i) $\frac{3}{4}$ j) $\frac{2}{5}$ k) $\frac{7}{10}$ l) $\frac{1}{100}$

3. a) 20% b) 15% c) 35% d) 60%
  e) 50% f) 30% g) 75% h) 90%
  i) 85% j) 10% k) 5% l) 70%

4. a) 0.3 b) 0.45 c) 0.65 d) 0.8
  e) 0.9 f) 0.25 g) 0.05 h) 0.15
  i) 0.3 j) 0.55 k) 0.35 l) 0.85

5. a) 15%, 20%, 25%, $\frac{9}{25}$, $\frac{6}{10}$, $\frac{4}{5}$

  b) 10%, $\frac{1}{4}$, 40%, $\frac{23}{50}$, 60%, $\frac{7}{10}$

  c) $\frac{1}{50}$, 3%, $\frac{1}{10}$, $\frac{3}{20}$, 16%, 50%

Pages 34–35

1. a) $0.7 \times 5 = 3.5$ b) $0.8 \times 3 = 2.4$
  c) $2.4 \times 6 = 14.4$ d) $1.4 \times 9 = 12.6$
  e) $2.3 \times 8 = 18.4$ f) $4.1 \times 5 = 20.5$
  g) $0.9 \times 5 = 4.5$ h) $1.8 \times 6 = 10.8$

2. a) 4.5 b) 3.6 c) 5.6 d) 9.2
  e) 7.1 f) 10.3

3. a) 4.4 b) 0.8 c) 5.4 d) 1.4
  e) 2.5 f) 4.8

4. a) $\mathbf{0.3} \times 6 = 1.8$
  b) $3.4 \times 7 = \mathbf{2}3.8$
  c) $\mathbf{1}.9 \times 5 = 9.\mathbf{5}$
  d) $2.6 \times 4 = 10.\mathbf{4}$

Pages 36–37

1. a) 64 b) 121
  c) 49 d) 36
  e) 81 f) 100
  g) 25 h) 144

2. 9, 25, 49, 64, 81, 100, 121, 144

3. The square numbers are all in a diagonal line.

4. a) 4 b) 9 c) 16 d) 25
  e) 36 f) 49 g) 64 h) 81
  i) 100

5. They are all square numbers.

Pages 38–39

1. a) 15 cm², 16 cm b) 24 cm², 20 cm
  c) 25 cm², 20 cm d) 18 cm², 18 cm
  e) 36 cm², 24 cm f) 32 cm², 24 cm

2. Area column should be completed as follows:
36, 40, 48, 49, 40, 45, 52, 100, 54, 121, 64, 400
Perimeter column should be completed as follows:
30, 28, 28, 28, 26, 36, 34, 50, 42, 44, 40, 80

3. a) 4 cm b) 16 cm
4. a) 9 cm b) 81 cm²

Pages 40–41

1. a) 6.05 p.m. b) 9.15 a.m. c) 10.30 a.m.
  d) 3.35 p.m. e) 8.55 p.m.

2. a) 8.15 a.m. b) 1 hour 45 minutes (or $1\frac{3}{4}$ hours)
  c) 4 hours 50 minutes d) 11.50 a.m.
  e) 6.15 a.m.

3. a) Bus D b) Bus B

Page 42

1. 50%
2. 13.6
3. 54.32
4. 24%, $\frac{7}{25}$
5. $\frac{3}{10}$
6. 0.8, $\frac{4}{5}$
7. <
8. 0.73
9. 12.8
10. 5.29 kg, 0.925 kg
11. >
12. 90%
13. 87
14. 4.2, 4.0 (or 4)
15. 2.8
16. 0.12
17. 0.65
18. 6.19
19. 1.5, 1.6
20. 0.5

Page 43

1. 16
2. 12 m²
3. 4.05 p.m.
4. Area = 32 cm²;
  Perimeter = 24 cm
5. 1 hour 25 minutes
6. 7 cm
7. 11.40 a.m.
8. 81
9. 80 cm
10. 10 cm
11. 36
12. 1 hour 40 minutes
13. Area = 27 cm²;
  Perimeter = 24 cm
14. 6.10 p.m.
15. 144
16. 8 cm
17. 25
18. Saturday
19. 45 minutes
20. Sunday

2 Change these mixed numbers to improper fractions.

a) $2\frac{1}{4}$ = $\frac{8}{4}$ **b)** $4\frac{1}{3}$ =

c) $1\frac{5}{8}$ =   **d)** $3\frac{3}{4}$ =

e) $2\frac{2}{5}$ =   **f)** $1\frac{1}{6}$ =

3 Change these improper fractions to mixed numbers.

a) $\frac{3}{2}$ =   **b)** $\frac{5}{4}$ =

c) $\frac{10}{3}$ =   **d)** $\frac{8}{7}$ =

e) $\frac{15}{2}$ =   **f)** $\frac{16}{3}$ =

4 Write the fraction each arrow points to as a mixed number **and** as an improper fraction.

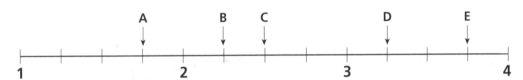

5 Write these fractions in order, starting with the smallest.

$\left(\frac{14}{4}\right)$ $\left(\frac{12}{4}\right)$ $\left(4\frac{1}{2}\right)$

 $3\frac{2}{4}$ 3

     $\left(3\frac{3}{4}\right)$ $\left(2\frac{1}{4}\right)$ $\left(\frac{11}{2}\right)$

     $5\frac{1}{2}$

How did you do?

23

Fractions of amounts

When you have a number of the same item, these can be divided into fractions of amounts.

Example: Here are 20 oranges.

Which would give you the greatest number of oranges?
$\frac{1}{5}$ of 20 or $\frac{1}{2}$ of 20 or $\frac{1}{4}$ of 20?

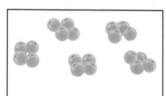

Five groups

$\frac{1}{5}$ of 20 = 4

Two groups

$\frac{1}{2}$ of 20 = 10

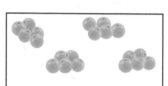

Four groups

$\frac{1}{4}$ of 20 = 5

$\frac{1}{2}$ is greater than $\frac{1}{4}$ and $\frac{1}{4}$ is greater than $\frac{1}{5}$. $\frac{1}{2} > \frac{1}{4} > \frac{1}{5}$

Warm up

1 Choose the circled fraction that gives the largest amount. Use the pictures to help.

a) 18 balls

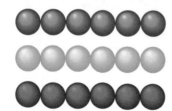

$\left(\frac{1}{6}\right) < \left(\frac{1}{3}\right)$

b) 16 balls

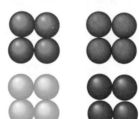

$\left(\frac{1}{4}\right) < \left(\frac{1}{2}\right)$

c) 21 balls

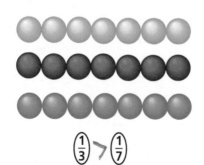

$\left(\frac{1}{3}\right) > \left(\frac{1}{7}\right)$

d) 18 balls

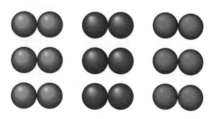

$\left(\frac{1}{6}\right) > \left(\frac{1}{9}\right)$

2 Complete by writing < or > between each pair of amounts.

a) $\frac{2}{3}$ of 90 ☐ $\frac{7}{10}$ of 90   b) $\frac{3}{4}$ of 100 ☐ $\frac{4}{5}$ of 100

c) $\frac{3}{10}$ of 140 ☐ $\frac{2}{7}$ of 140   d) $\frac{5}{8}$ of 160 ☐ $\frac{3}{4}$ of 160

3 Answer these questions.

a) **What fraction of £1 is:**	b) **What fraction of £2 is:**	c) **What fraction of £10 is:**
50p	20p	£2.50
20p	£1	£5
10p	50p	£1
25p	£1.50	£7.50
75p	40p	£2

4 Read and answer these questions.

a) Would it be lighter to carry $\frac{1}{5}$ of 10 kg or $\frac{1}{10}$ of 10 kg?

b) Joy wants a large slice of cake. Should she cut the cake into quarters or thirds to get a larger slice?

c) There are 24 hours in a day. Peter spends a quarter of the day at school and a third asleep. Does he spend more time at school or more time sleeping?

d) There are 45 fish. $\frac{3}{5}$ are spotted and $\frac{2}{9}$ are striped. Are there more striped or more spotted fish?

 **How did you do?**

Fraction calculations

Remember that to add and subtract fractions with the same denominator, just add or subtract the numerators.

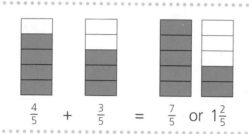

$$\frac{4}{5} + \frac{3}{5} = \frac{7}{5} \text{ or } 1\frac{2}{5}$$

If it is a mixed number, change it to an improper fraction.

$$1\frac{2}{5} - \frac{3}{5} = \underline{\quad} \qquad \frac{7}{5} - \frac{3}{5} = \frac{4}{5}$$

To add or subtract fractions with different denominators, convert to equivalent fractions so both have the same denominator. Then add or subtract the numerators.

$$\frac{2}{5} + \frac{3}{10} = \underline{\quad}$$

Convert $\frac{2}{5}$ to tenths so the denominators are the same.

$$\frac{2}{5} = \frac{4}{10}$$

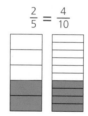

$$\frac{4}{10} + \frac{3}{10} = \frac{7}{10} \quad \text{so} \quad \frac{2}{5} + \frac{3}{10} = \frac{7}{10}$$

Warm up

1 Write the pairs of fractions that total 3.

$\left(1\frac{3}{4}\right)$ $\left(\frac{2}{3}\right)$ $\left(1\frac{7}{8}\right)$ $\left(\frac{7}{10}\right)$ $\left(1\frac{1}{8}\right)$

$\left(2\frac{3}{10}\right)$ $\left(2\frac{1}{3}\right)$ $\left(1\frac{1}{3}\right)$ $\left(1\frac{1}{4}\right)$ $\left(1\frac{2}{3}\right)$

2 Subtract these fractions.

a) $\frac{9}{4} - \frac{1}{4} =$ b) $\frac{7}{10} - \frac{1}{10} =$ c) $\frac{12}{5} - \frac{3}{5} =$ d) $\frac{11}{10} - \frac{3}{10} =$

3 Add together the shaded parts of these shapes. Give your answers as fractions **and** mixed numbers.

a)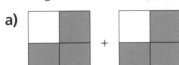

b)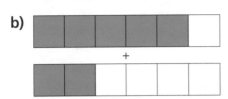

c)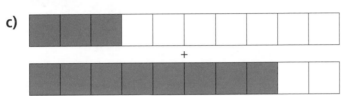

d)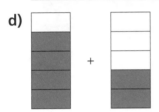

4 Subtract these fractions. Change mixed numbers to improper fractions to make them easier to work out.

a) $1\frac{1}{4} - \frac{3}{4} =$

b) $1\frac{1}{3} - \frac{2}{3} =$

5 Answer these fraction calculations.

a) $\frac{3}{5} + \frac{1}{10} =$

b) $\frac{7}{8} - \frac{3}{4} =$

6 Answer these.

a) Add together $\frac{1}{4}$ and $6\frac{3}{4}$.

b) What is the difference between $1\frac{3}{10}$ m and $\frac{7}{10}$ m?

c) What is the sum of $\frac{5}{9}$ and $\frac{1}{3}$?

d) How much more is $\frac{11}{12}$ litres than $\frac{1}{2}$ a litre?

How did you do?

Progress test 3

1. What is the next prime number after 13?

2. $49 \div 7 =$

3. Write the missing pair of factors for 18.

   (1, 18) (2, 9) (_____ , _____)

4. Answer these multiplications.

   $9 \times 6 =$

   $90 \times 60 =$

5. $28 \times 5 =$

6. Answer this, writing the remainder as a decimal.

   $55 \div 2 =$ _____

7. $8800 \div 11 =$ _____ r _____

8. Which number is **not** a prime number?

   ㉑   ㊶
   ⑪   ㉛

9. Work out the missing factor for 16.

   1, 2, _____ , 8, 16

10. $40 \times 70 =$

11. Which number is a common multiple of 5 and 3?

    $\boxed{40}$
    $\boxed{70}$ $\boxed{60}$

12. $36 \div 12 =$

13. $53 \times 7 =$

14. What is the remainder when 58 is divided by 6?

15. Copy and write < or > between these two calculations to make this correct.

    8×24 $\square$ 2×84

16. Multiply these three numbers.

    $\boxed{8}$ $\boxed{3}$ $\boxed{5}$

17. Answer this, writing the remainder as a fraction.

    $72 \div 5 =$ _____

Look at these numbers for questions 18–20.

   4   8   5   12

---

18. Which number is a multiple of 3?

19. Which number is **not** a factor of 60?

20. Which number is a factor of 52?

Score ⬭/ 20

1 $\frac{1}{6}$ of 24 =

2 What fraction of £5 is £1.25?

3 Which **two** fractions total 5?

 $1\frac{1}{2}$

$4\frac{1}{2}$

$2\frac{1}{2}$

$3\frac{1}{2}$

4 Write this as an **improper fraction** and a **mixed number**.

5 $\frac{14}{4} - \frac{3}{4} =$

6 Write $2\frac{7}{10}$ as an improper fraction.

7 What is the smallest fraction?
What is the greatest fraction?

$\frac{7}{3}$ $1\frac{2}{3}$ $\frac{8}{3}$ $1\frac{1}{3}$ $\frac{6}{3}$

8 Add together $\frac{1}{3}$ and $4\frac{2}{3}$.

9 Write these fractions in order, smallest first.

$\frac{1}{10}$ $\frac{1}{2}$ $\frac{1}{7}$ $\frac{1}{4}$

10 Which **two** fractions have the same value?

$1\frac{4}{5}$ $3\frac{1}{5}$ $\frac{13}{5}$

$\frac{14}{5}$ $\frac{9}{5}$ $1\frac{3}{5}$

11 Add these together and write the answer as an **improper fraction** and a **mixed number**. Use the shaded shapes to help you.

+

$\frac{2}{6} + \frac{5}{6} =$

12 $\frac{1}{8}$ of 72 =

13 $1\frac{2}{9} - \frac{4}{9} =$

14 How much is $\frac{1}{5}$ of £1?

15 Write the fraction at the arrow as an **improper fraction** and a **mixed number**.

16 Write the answer to this fraction addition as an **improper fraction** and a **mixed number**.

$\frac{8}{9} + \frac{6}{9} =$

17 In a bag of 30 balloons, $\frac{3}{10}$ are pink and $\frac{2}{5}$ are blue. Which are there more of, pink or blue balloons?

18 Write $\frac{5}{3}$ as a mixed number.

19 $\frac{7}{10}$ of 120 =

20 Write **<** or **>** to make this true.

$\frac{7}{10}$ of 40 ☐ $\frac{4}{5}$ of 40

Score ⬤/20

29

Decimals

Follow these rules for multiplying and dividing numbers by 10 and 100.

To multiply by 10

Move the digits one place to the left.

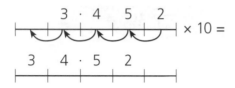

To multiply by 100

Move the digits two places to the left.

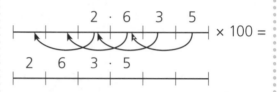

To divide by 10

Move the digits one place to the right.

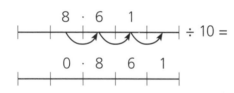

To divide by 100

Move the digits two places to the right.

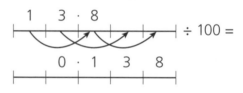

Predict how you would multiply and divide by 1000.

Warm up

1 Multiply these by 10 and write the answers.

a) $0.34 \times 10 =$ b) $8.6 \times 10 =$ c) $1.228 \times 10 =$

d) $0.855 \times 10 =$ e) $3.72 \times 10 =$ f) $1.62 \times 10 =$

2 Divide these by 10 and write the answers.

a) $83.5 \div 10 =$ b) $19 \div 10 =$ c) $227.6 \div 10 =$

d) $28.45 \div 10 =$ e) $0.93 \div 10 =$ f) $12.84 \div 10 =$

3 Multiply these by 100 and write the answers.

a) 3.68 × 100 =   b) 0.3 × 100 =

c) 1.005 × 100 =   d) 2.934 × 100 =

e) 0.655 × 100 =   f) 46.385 × 100 =

4 Divide these by 100 and write the answers.

a) 27 ÷ 100 =   b) 342 ÷ 100 =

c) 53.8 ÷ 100 =   d) 6.3 ÷ 100 =

e) 27.9 ÷ 100 =   f) 145.2 ÷ 100 =

5 Write these masses in order starting with the lightest.

8.245 kg   0.95 kg   8.3 kg   0.855 kg

8.455 kg   8.52 kg

Challenge yourself

6 Round each decimal number to the nearest tenth. Use the number line to help you.

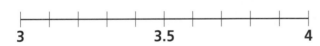

3   3.5   4

a) 3.25   b) 3.83
c) 3.08   d) 3.57
e) 3.90   f) 3.35

How did you do?

Fractions, decimals and percentages

A **percentage** is a fraction with a denominator of 100.

To express a fraction as a percentage, change it to an equivalent fraction with a denominator of 100, e.g.

$$\frac{2}{5} = \frac{40}{100} = 40\%$$

To express a percentage as a fraction, change it to a fraction with a denominator of 100 and reduce the fraction to its simplest form, e.g.

$$25\% = \frac{25}{100} = \frac{1}{4}$$

To express a decimal as a percentage, multiply the decimal by 100, e.g.

$$0.2 = 20\%$$

To express a percentage as a decimal, divide the percentage by 100, e.g.

$$60\% = 0.6$$

Warm up

1 Write each of these fractions as a percentage.

a) $\frac{1}{2}$ = _____%

b) $\frac{1}{4}$ = _____%

c) $\frac{1}{10}$ = _____%

d) $\frac{1}{5}$ = _____%

e) $\frac{3}{5}$ = _____%

f) $\frac{18}{25}$ = _____%

g) $\frac{29}{50}$ = _____%

h) $\frac{13}{20}$ = _____%

i) $\frac{4}{5}$ = _____%

j) $\frac{3}{10}$ = _____%

k) $\frac{17}{50}$ = _____%

l) $\frac{11}{20}$ = _____%

Test yourself

2 Write each of these percentages as a fraction reduced to its simplest form.

a) 10% =

b) 80% =

c) 50% =

d) 30% =

e) 60% =

f) 25% =

g) 5% =

h) 90% =

i) 75% =

j) 40% =

k) 70% =

l) 1% =

3 Write each of these decimals as a percentage.

    a) 0.2 = _____%   **b)** 0.15 = _____%

    c) 0.35 = _____%   **d)** 0.6 = _____%

    e) 0.5 = _____%   **f)** 0.3 = _____%

    g) 0.75 = _____%   **h)** 0.9 = _____%

    i) 0.85 = _____%   **j)** 0.1 = _____%

    k) 0.05 = _____%   **l)** 0.7 = _____%

4 Write each of these percentages as a decimal.

    a) 30% =   **b)** 45% =

    c) 65% =   **d)** 80% =

    e) 90% =   **f)** 25% =

    g) 5% =   **h)** 15% =

    i) 30% =   **j)** 55% =

    k) 35% =   **l)** 85% =

Challenge yourself

5 Order these fractions and percentages from smallest to largest.
You may find it helpful to change all the fractions to percentages.

    a) $\frac{4}{5}$ 15%   25% $\frac{9}{25}$ 20% $\frac{6}{10}$

    b) 40% $\frac{23}{50}$ $\frac{1}{4}$ 10% $\frac{7}{10}$ 60%

    c) 3% $\frac{3}{20}$ 50% $\frac{1}{10}$ 16% $\frac{1}{50}$

How did you do?

Decimal calculations

Use facts you know to calculate with decimals. Look at the numbers and decide on the best strategy to work out the answer.

Use near doubles.

Example: What is 3.6 + 3.5?

$$3.5 + 3.5 = 7$$

So, 3.5 + 3.6 = 7.1

Count on or back in different jumps.

Example: What is 9.2 − 6.8?

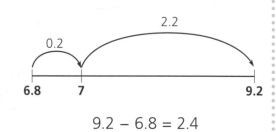

$$9.2 - 6.8 = 2.4$$

Partition, or break numbers up.

Example: What is 4.8 × 5?

$$4 \times 5 = 20$$
$$0.8 \times 5 = 4$$

So, 4.8 × 5 = 24

Use facts you know.

Example: What is 0.9 × 7?

$$9 \times 7 = 63$$

So, 0.9 × 7 = 6.3

Warm up

1. Choose the correct decimal answer from the box for each of these calculations.

| 3.5 | 2.4 | 12.6 | 10.8 | 14.4 | 18.4 | 4.5 | 20.5 |

a) 0.7 × 5

b) 0.8 × 3

c) 2.4 × 6

d) 1.4 × 9

e) 2.3 × 8

f) 4.1 × 5

g) 0.9 × 5

h) 1.8 × 6

2 Answer these.

a) 0.6 + 3.9 =   **b)** 2.8 + 0.8 =   **c)** 4.7 + 0.9 =

d) 6.8 + 2.4 =   **e)** 5.4 + 1.7 =   **f)** 7.5 + 2.8 =

3 Picture the jumps on these number lines to help you subtract mentally.

a) 7.8 − 3.4 =

b) 2.5 − 1.7 =

c) 8.9 − 3.5 =

d) 4.2 − 2.8 =

e) 9.4 − 6.9 =

f) 7.4 − 2.6 =

4 Copy and complete the missing digits, 0–5, in these calculations.

| 0 | 1 | 2 | 3 | 4 | 5 |

a) ☐.☐ × 6 = 1.8   **b)** 3.4 × 7 = ☐ 3.8

c) ☐.9 × 5 = 9.☐   **d)** 2.6 × 4 = 1 0.☐

How did you do?

Square numbers

Look at this pattern.

1   4   9   16

The numbers 1, 4, 9 and 16 are examples of **square numbers**, when two identical whole numbers are multiplied together.

1 squared is written as 1^2.

$1^2 \longrightarrow 1 \times 1 = 1$

$2^2 \longrightarrow 2 \times 2 = 4$

$3^2 \longrightarrow 3 \times 3 = 9$

$4^2 \longrightarrow 4 \times 4 = 16$

Warm up

1 Answer these to find more square numbers.

    a) $8^2 =$ **b)** $11^2 =$

    c) $7^2 =$ **d)** $6^2 =$

    e) $9^2 =$ **f)** $10^2 =$

    g) $5^2 =$ **h)** $12^2 =$

2 Copy and complete this set of square numbers.

    1   4 ___ 16 ___ 36 ___ ___ ___ ___ ___ ___

3 Put counters or small pieces of paper on all the square numbers. Describe what you notice.

×	1	2	3	4	5	6	7	8	9	10	11	12
1	1	2	3	4	5	6	7	8	9	10	11	12
2	2	4	6	8	10	12	14	16	18	20	22	24
3	3	6	9	12	15	18	21	24	27	30	33	36
4	4	8	12	16	20	24	28	32	36	40	44	48
5	5	10	15	20	25	30	35	40	45	50	55	60
6	6	12	18	24	30	36	42	48	54	60	66	72
7	7	14	21	28	35	42	49	56	63	70	77	84
8	8	16	24	32	40	48	56	64	72	80	88	96
9	9	18	27	36	45	54	63	72	81	90	99	108
10	10	20	30	40	50	60	70	80	90	100	110	120
11	11	22	33	44	55	66	77	88	99	110	121	132
12	12	24	36	48	60	72	84	96	108	120	132	144

4 Add these consecutive odd numbers and write the total.

a) 1 + 3 =   **b)** 1 + 3 + 5 =

c) 1 + 3 + 5 + 7 =   **d)** 1 + 3 + 5 + 7 + 9 =

e) 1 + 3 + 5 + 7 + 9 + 11 =   **f)** 1 + 3 + 5 + 7 + 9 + 11 + 13 =

g) 1 + 3 + 5 + 7 + 9 + 11 + 13 + 15 =   **h)** 1 + 3 + 5 + 7 + 9 + 11 + 13 + 15 + 17 =

i) 1 + 3 + 5 + 7 + 9 + 11 + 13 + 15 + 17 + 19 =

5 Look at your answers for question 4 above. What do you notice about them?

How did you do?

Area and perimeter

The **area** is the amount of space taken up on a flat surface.

The area of this rectangle is 30 square centimetres or 30 cm^2. It can be calculated by multiplying the length by the width.

Area = 6 cm × 5 cm = 30 cm^2

Area of rectangle = Length × Width $A = L \times W$

6 cm

5 cm

The **perimeter** is the distance all the way around a shape. Add together the length of each side of the rectangle.

Perimeter of rectangle = 2 × (Length + Width) $P = 2 \times (L + W)$

6 cm + 6 cm + 5 cm + 5 cm = 22 cm

Perimeter = 22 cm

Warm up

1 Work out the area and perimeter of each of these shapes.

a) 3 cm

5 cm
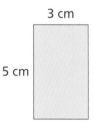

b) 4 cm

6 cm
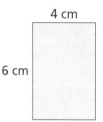

c) 5 cm

5 cm
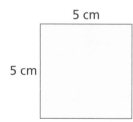

d) 3 cm

6 cm
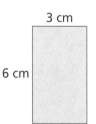

e) 6 cm

6 cm
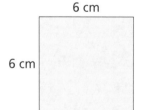

f) 4 cm

8 cm
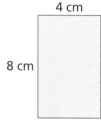

2 This table shows the length and width of different rectangles.
Calculate the area and perimeter of each rectangle.

Length L	Width W	Area (cm²) L × W	Perimeter (cm) 2 × (L + W)
12 cm	3 cm		
4 cm	10 cm		
6 cm	8 cm		
7 cm	7 cm		
5 cm	8 cm		
15 cm	3 cm		
4 cm	13 cm		
20 cm	5 cm		
18 cm	3 cm		
11 cm	11 cm		
16 cm	4 cm		
20 cm	20 cm		

Challenge yourself

3 The area of a square is 16 cm².

a) What is the length of each side?

b) What is the perimeter of the square?

4 The perimeter of a square is 36 cm.

a) What is the length of each side?

b) What is the area of the square?

How did you do?

Time

The **duration** of an event is how much time it takes. A timeline is very useful to help work this out.

Example: A film starts at 6.40 p.m. and finishes at 8.15 p.m. How long does the film last?

Use a timeline and count on from the start to the finish:

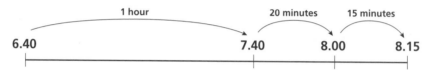

1 hour + 20 minutes + 15 minutes is 1 hour 35 minutes.

So the film lasts for 1 hour 35 minutes.

Warm up

1 Write the time that is:

a) 40 minutes later than 5.25 p.m.

b) 25 minutes later than 8.50 a.m.

c) 20 minutes earlier than 10.50 a.m.

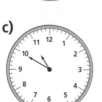

d) 45 minutes earlier than 4.20 p.m.

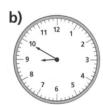

e) 1 hour 10 minutes later than 7.45 p.m.

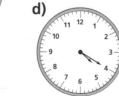

40

2 Answer these questions.

a) It takes Ben 35 minutes to walk to school.

If he arrives at 8.50 a.m., at what time does he leave home?

b) Jim drove a lorry from 6.55 a.m. until 8.40 a.m. before taking a rest.

How long had he been driving for?

c) A market stall opens at 8.15 a.m. and closes at 1.05 p.m.

How long is the stall open for?

d) David ran a half-marathon and finished in 1 hour 35 minutes.

If the race started at 10.15 a.m., what time did he finish?

e) Alice falls asleep at 8.50 p.m. and sleeps for 9 hours 25 minutes.

What time does she wake up?

Challenge yourself

3 Look at this bus timetable.

	Bus A	Bus B	Bus C	Bus D
School	8.15 a.m.	9.35 a.m.	11.05 a.m.	1.55 p.m.
Hospital	8.35 a.m.	9.50 a.m.	11.30 a.m.	2.15 p.m.
Market	8.45 a.m.	10.00 a.m.	11.40 a.m.	2.35 p.m.
Town Centre	9.10 a.m.	10.30 a.m.	12.05 p.m.	2.45 p.m.

a) Which is the fastest bus from the school to the town centre?

b) Which is the slowest bus from the hospital to the town centre?

How did you do?

1 $\frac{1}{2} = $ _____%

2 6.8 × 2 =

3 5.432 × 10 =

4 What is the smallest fraction or percentage in this set? What is the largest fraction or percentage in this set?

$\left(\frac{13}{50}\right)$ (25%) $\left(\frac{7}{25}\right)$

(24%) $\left(\frac{1}{4}\right)$ (27%)

5 Write 30% as a fraction in its simplest form.

6 Work out the missing digits.

$$80\% = 0.\underline{\quad} = \frac{\square}{5}$$

7 Write < or > between these two measurements to make this true.

4.119 km $\square$ 4.19 km

8 73 ÷ 100 =

9 3.2 × 4 =

10 What is the heaviest weight? What is the lightest weight?

(5.2 kg)   (5.29 kg)   (2.995 kg)

(5.02 kg)   (0.925 kg)

11 Write < or > between the percentage and the decimal number to make this true.

30% $\square$ 0.03

12 0.9 = _____%

13 0.87 × 100 =

14 Round each decimal to the nearest tenth.

4.17   4.017

15 4 × 0.7 =

16 12 ÷ 100 =

17 Write 65% as a decimal.

18 61.9 ÷ 10 =

19 Round these to the nearest tenth.

1.508   1.58

20 Picture the jumps on this number line to help you work out this subtraction.

1.7   2.2

2.2 − 1.7 =

Score $\bigcirc$ / 20

1 $4^2 =$

2 What is the area of a room in the shape of a rectangle with sides 3 m wide and 4 m long?

3 What time is 45 minutes later than 3.20 p.m.?

4 Work out the area and perimeter of this shape.

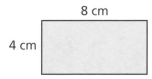

8 cm

4 cm

5 A film starts at 7.15 p.m. and finishes at 8.40 p.m. How long is the film?

6 The perimeter of a square is 28 cm. What is the length of each side?

7 Shobna's dance class starts at 10.10 a.m. and lasts for 1 hour 30 minutes. What time does the dance class finish?

8 $9^2 =$

9 What is the perimeter of a photo frame in the shape of a rectangle with sides 15 cm wide and 25 cm long?

10 The area of a square is 100 cm². What is the length of each side?

11 Which is the square number?

48   55

36   60

12 How long is 55 minutes and 45 minutes in total?

13 Work out the area and perimeter of this shape.

9 cm

3 cm

14 A bus leaves at 5.30 p.m., drives 15 minutes to the doctor's and drives another 25 minutes to the bus station. What time does it arrive at the bus station?

15 $12^2 =$

16 The area of a square is 64 cm². What is the length of each side?

17 What is the next square number?

4   9   16

These are the times of a TV show *Maths Fun!* Use this information to help you answer questions 18–20.

Maths Fun!	Saturday	Sunday
Starts	11.40 a.m.	4.55 p.m.
Finishes	12.25 p.m.	6.10 p.m.

18 On which day is *Maths Fun!* on TV in the morning?

19 How long is the Saturday *Maths Fun!* show?

20 Which is the longer *Maths Fun!* show, Saturday or Sunday?

Published by Keen Kite Books
An imprint of HarperCollins*Publishers* Ltd
The News Building
1 London Bridge Street
London SE1 9GF

ISBN 9780008161248

Text © 2013 Paul Broadbent and 2015 Keen Kite Books, an imprint of HarperCollins*Publishers* Ltd

Design © 2015 Keen Kite Books, an imprint of HarperCollins*Publishers* Ltd

The author asserts his moral right to be identified as the author of this work.